ides

ces

Wo f the World

Make the most of your time on Earth

25 YEARS 1982–2007

NEW YORK • LONDON • DELHI

Contents

Introduction

EXPERIENCES have always been at the heart of the Rough Guide concept. A group of us began writing the books **25 years ago** (hence this celebratory mini series) and wanted to share the kind of travels we had been doing ourselves. It seems bizarre to recall that in the early 1980s, travel was very much a minority pursuit. Sure, there was a lot of tourism around, and that was reflected in the guidebooks in print, which traipsed around the established sights with scarcely a backward look at the local population and their life. We wanted to change all that: to put a country or a city's popular culture centre stage, to highlight the clubs where you could hear local music, drink with people you hadn't come on holiday with, watch the local football, join in with the festivals. And of course we wanted to push travel a bit further, inspire readers with the confidence and knowledge to break away from established routes, to find pleasure and excitement in remote islands, or desert routes, or mountain treks, or in street culture.

Twenty-five years on, that thinking seems pretty obvious: we all want to experience something real about a destination, and to seek out travel's **ultimate experiences**. Which is exactly where these **25 books** come in. They are not in any sense a new series of guidebooks. We're happy with the series that we already have in print. Instead, the **25s** are a collection of ideas, enthusiasms and inspirations: a selection of the very best things to see or do – and not just before you die, but now. Each selection is gold dust. That's the brief to our writers: there is no room here for the average, no space fillers. Pick any one of our selections and you will enrich your travelling life.

But first of all, take the time to browse. Grab a half dozen of these books and let the ideas percolate ... and then begin making your plans.

Mark Ellingham
Founder & Series Editor, Rough Guides

Ultimate experiences Wonders of the World

01 A Salt on the Senses: Salar de Uyuni

"it feels like you're in an expensive car advert as you roll silently across the crystals"

Standing on the deserted streets of Uyuni, a dusty, windswept pueblo in remotest Bolivia, it's hard to imagine that a little under 15km away lies one of the world's most incredible natural phenomenons. A short, bumpy jeep ride to the west is the edge of the Salar de Uyuni, a vast expanse of salt flats that covers over 10,000 square kilometres of the country's southwestern corner like a giant coat of whitewash.

Bolivia lays claim to some of South America's finest natural attractions – the Amazon, the Pantanal and Lake Titicaca all lie within its borders – but for sheer stop-you-in-your-tracks surrealism, the Salar de Uyuni is in a class of its own. The clarity of the altiplano sky is startling, the juxtaposition between blazing blue and sparkling white remarkable, and it feels like you're in an expensive car advert as you roll silently across the crystals, with only the Isla del Pescado, a cacti-studded island in a sea of salt, breaking the bleached horizon.

The salar's origins vary depending on who you ask: geologists will tell you it was formed either by the drying up of an enormous lake into which salt had been washed from surrounding land, deposited when what is now Bolivia was under the ocean; locals will have you believe it came into being when Yana Pollera, the mountain goddess, flooded the southwestern plains with her milk so that her child, Kaliktan, could feed – the milk eventually turning into salt. It's hard not to wonder if the locals aren't onto something, such is the bizarreness of it all. Stepping from the jeep, the ground crunching underfoot as if it were hard-packed snow, it's just salt, salt and more salt as far as the eye can see, like a million diamonds twinkling in the southern sun.

need to know

The only way to visit the Salar de Uyuni is on an organized tour from Uyuni, a twelve-hour bus ride from La Paz. Tours are by 4WD and last three or four days, taking in the salt flats, as well as the Reserva de Fauna Andina Eduardo Avaroa, a wildlife reserve of glacial green and red lakes on the border with Chile.

ROCK STEADY: admiring the shifting shades of Uluru

Lounging on one of its pristine beaches, it's easy to forget that most of Australia is a vast wilderness of flat, sun-scorched earth, an ancient outback populated by a few hardy farmers and the continent's Aboriginal peoples. At its heart, marooned in an endless desert of Mulga scrub and hummock grass, lies the colossal red monolith of Uluru, also known as Ayer's Rock after Sir Henry Ayers, the chief secretary of South Australia when Europeans "discovered" it in the 1870s.

Its different names reflect a split personality: Ayer's Rock is testimony to the power of global tourism, clambered over, photographed from every angle from sunrise to sunset, and viewed by plane, bus and helicopter; Uluru is also the sacred place of the Aboriginal Anangu people, alive with myth and magical power. You can climb Ayer's Rock, or sip champagne, eat vast barbecues and have breakfast while admiring it. But as you do so be aware that Uluru is littered with marks, gullies and bumps that represent tribal creation stories, a trove of ancient knowledge that sums up the Anangu concept of *tjukurpa*.

In truth, it's hard not to experience a little of both, whatever your preference. Protected within the Uluru-Kata Tjuta National Park, Uluru is owned by the Anangu and leased back to the government. The park's bright Cultural Centre sheds light on their belief systems and stories, while their tours take you close to – but not onto – the rock, and put it into an Aboriginal context.

In the end, it's impossible not to be captivated simply by its sheer size. The Anangu plead with visitors not to climb it, but they have never tried to enforce a ban. And although the carnival of tour buses and jeeps that assemble every morning and late afternoon to snap the rock's colourful transformation at sunrise and sunset can be off-putting, watching the sandstone's chameleon-like change – from a thousand shades of earthy golds and ochres, to pinks and copper-tones, and, finally, a deep, ruby-red – is truly unforgettable.

need to know

Uluru is served by Connellan Airport, with daily flights to most cities in Australia, and the purpose-built resort of Yulara contains a range of accommodation to suit most budgets, just outside the park. Entrance to the Uluru-Kata Tjuta National Park (daily: June & July 6.30am–7.30pm, Dec–Feb 5am–9pm) costs AU$25. The Cultural Centre is open daily 7am–6pm (free with park entrance). Aboriginal guided tours are run by Anangu Tours (ⓦwww.ananguwaai.com.au), and depart daily from the Cultural Centre one hour before sunrise, include breakfast and take 4–4.5 hours (AU$119 per person).

The PYRAMIDS of GIZA

The Pyramids at Giza were built at the very beginning of recorded human history, and for nearly five millennia they have stood on the edge of the desert plateau in magnificent communion with the sky.

Not only are the Pyramids on the edge of the desert, these days they are on the edge of the city, and it must be a strange experience indeed to look out of the windows of the nearby tower blocks each day to a view like this. The closest, the Great Pyramid, contains the tomb of Cheops, the Fourth Dynasty pharaoh who ruled Egypt during the Old Kingdom. This is the oldest of the group, built in about 2570 BC, and the largest – in fact it's the most massive single monument on the face of the earth today. The others, built by Cheops' son Chephren and his grandson Mycerinus, stand in descending order of age and size along a southwest axis; when built they were probably aligned precisely with the North Star, their entrance corridors aiming straight at it.

You can enter the Great Pyramid through a hole hacked into its north face in the ninth century AD by the caliph Mamun who was hunting for buried treasure. Crouching through low and narrow passages you arrive at the Great Gallery which ascends through the heart of the pyramid to Cephren's burial chamber. You are likely to have the chamber to yourself, as claustrophobia and difficulty for some in breathing due to inadequate oxygen mean that few people come this far. Occasionally visitors are accidentally locked in overnight.

The overwhelming impression made by the pyramids is due not only to the magnitude of their age and size, but also to their elemental form, their simple but compelling triangular silhouettes against the sky. The best way to enjoy this is to hire a horse or camel and ride about the desert, seeing them from different angles, from close up and looming, or far off and standing lonely but defiantly on the open sands. The best times to do it are at dawn, at sunset and at night when they form as much a part of the natural order as the sun, the moon and the stars.

need to know

The Pyramids are 11km west of Cairo and can be reached by the #355 bus from the Egyptian Museum. The site is open daily from 6.30am to midnight in summer, from 7am to 8pm in winter. Horses and camels are offered by local Bedouin; the tourist office will tell you the official rates of hire.

04 Drifting down THE AMAZON

Of all the wonders of South America, none captures the imagination perhaps as much as the Amazon rainforest. Covering an area almost as large as the continental United States, and extending from Brazil into seven other countries, the Amazon basin is by far the most biologically diverse region on earth, home to an astonishing variety of plant and animal life – rare birds and mammals, extraordinary insects and reptiles, and literally millions of plant species – all woven together into a rich and complex natural tapestry.

Despite its immense size, the forest is disappearing at an alarming rate, and if you want to see the fabulous wildlife close up you need to head upstream by boat, taking either one of the many excursion boats or – better – a motorized dugout canoe. As you chug into the remote backwaters of the Amazon, every twist and turn offers the prospect of something to see: turtles or caiman crocodiles basking in the sun; pink river dolphins playing in the brown waters; flocks of brightly coloured macaws or toucans flying overhead; monkeys cavorting in the treetops on either side; and perhaps even a giant anteater drinking along the river bank.

For accommodation, you can camp out on the riverbank, with the nocturnal noise of the forest all around, or stay at one of a growing number of eco-lodges. Some of these are run by indigenous tribes, built in traditional style from natural materials harvested from the forest but with modern additions, such as solar-powered lighting. Staying with indigenous hosts gives an insight into cultures that have developed over many centuries of living in close harmony with the rainforest. You'll get a chance to sample traditional Amazonian food – minus the endangered animal species that are now hunted for photographs rather than food – and learn how people survive in a natural environment that to outsiders can seem extremely hostile. Best of all, you'll get to walk forest trails with an indigenous guide, and tap in to their encyclopaedic knowledge of the rainforest ecosystem. The guides may not know the scientific name of every species you encounter, but they can usually explain its behaviour, uses and place in local legend. In fact, many visitors find the lifestyle and culture of their Amazonian hosts as fascinating as any of the plants or animals they see in the rainforest.

need to know

Unless you've considerable wilderness experience and all your own equipment, the only way to explore the Amazon is on an organized tour or by hiring a local guide with a boat. Trips are easy to arrange in main towns like Manaus in Brazil, Iquitos in Peru or Rurrenabaque in Bolivia. Prices vary between countries but count on paying around $30 a day for an organized excursion, plus $50 or so to stay at an eco-lodge. The price of a local guide and canoe will be a lot lower, especially if you're sharing – fuel for the outboard motor is the main expense.

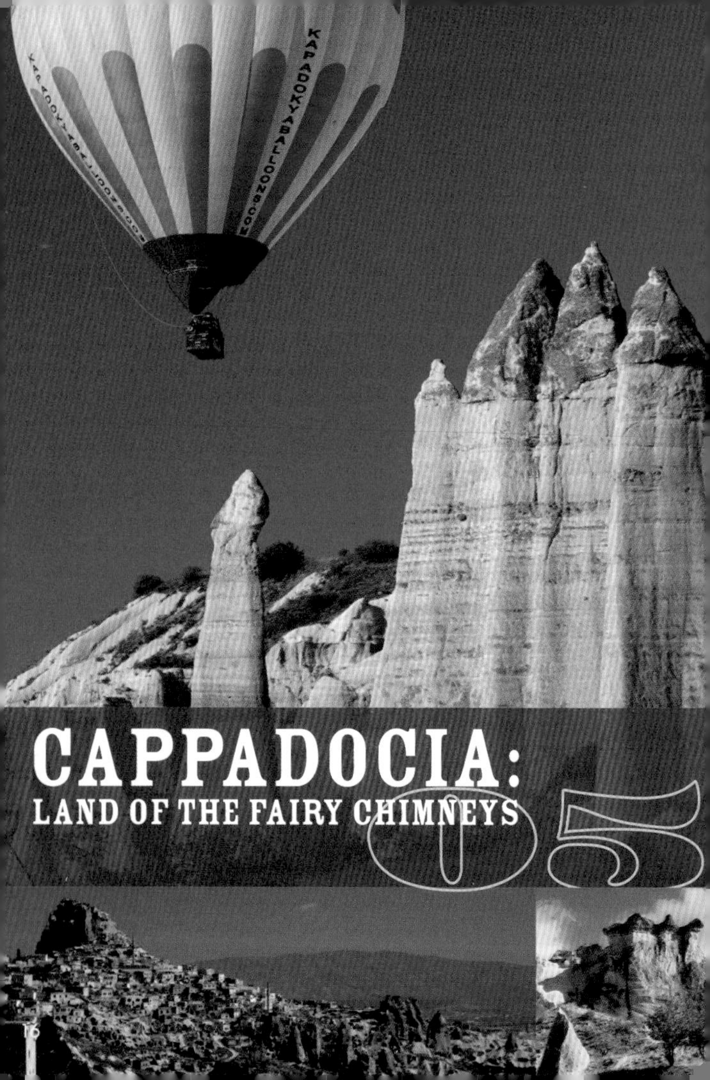

05 CAPPADOCIA: LAND OF THE FAIRY CHIMNEYS

An expanse of undulating, cave-pocked, tunnel-riddled rock at the centre of Turkey, Cappadocia is a landscape like no other. It's one of those rare places that can draw quality snaps from even the most slapdash photographer, with a rocky palette that shifts from terracotta through pink and honey to dazzling white, and the orange fires of sunrise and sunset adding their own hues to the mix. From Uçhisar's castle to the cliff-hewn churches of Çavusin, there are heavenly views at every turn: surreal stone towers up to fifty metres in height pop up along innumerable valleys: some resemble witches' hats, others are mushroom-shaped, a couple defy gravitational logic and a few are markedly phallic, but to locals they're all the *peribacalar* – or "Fairy Chimneys".

Though the countryside is ideal for hiking, cycling or an aimless ramble, there's no need to stay surface-bound. Delve below ground into one of many underground cities, built up to 4000 years ago and once home to whole squads of troglodytes, or float up in a balloon to watch the sun rise over the peaks. From on high you'll also see the entrances to thousands of caves which riddle the area like Swiss cheese – some towers are honeycombed with up to twenty cave-levels, hand-hewn from the rock hundreds of years ago. Before the tourist trade, the indentations found in many caves were used to harvest pigeon dung, which was then used as fertilizer in local fields. Other caverns, particularly those lining the green Ihlara Valley, served as churches to what was once a large Christian community. Although still host to the odd family, hermit or teashop, most of the caves lie empty, and some intrepid travellers save on accommodation costs by slinging their sleeping bags in out-of-the-way grottoes. However, in towns such as Çavusin and Ürgüp, or the relaxed backpacker capital of Göreme, there are a few caves that have been converted into comfy hotels and guesthouses. Head to Cappadocia and fall asleep in your very own cave.

need to know Göreme and Ürgüp have regular bus connections to cities all over Turkey, although the town of Nevsehir, 20km to the west, gets in the way, and you often get dropped here even if you have a ticket to Göreme; buses leaving Göreme may also have to stop in Nevsehir to connect with the main services.

LOST FOR WORDS AT the Grand Canyon

06

need to know Grand Canyon National Park ($25 per vehicle) lies in northern Arizona. The South Rim is open 24 hours a day, 365 days a year, while the North Rim is open from mid-May to mid-October.

If a guidebook tells you that something is "impossible to describe", it usually means the writer can't be bothered to describe it – with one exception. After pondering the views of the Grand Canyon for the first time, the most spectacular natural wonder on earth, most visitors are stunned into silence. Committed travellers hike down to the canyon floor on foot or by mule, spending a night at *Phantom Ranch*, or hover above in a helicopter to get a better grasp of its dimensions. But it is still hard to grasp. The problem isn't lack of words. It's just that the canyon is so vast and so deep, that the vista stretches so far across your line of vision, up, down and across, giving the impression of hundreds of miles of space, that it's a bit like looking at one of those puzzles in reverse – the more you stare, the more it becomes harder to work out what it is or where you are. Distance becomes meaningless, depth blurs, and your sense of time and space withers away.

The facts are similarly mind-boggling: Grand Canyon is around 277 miles long and one mile deep. The South Rim, where most of the tourists go, averages 7000 feet (2134m), while the North Rim is over 8000 feet high (2438m) – its alpine landscape only adding to the sense of the surreal. On the canyon floor flows the Colorado River, its waters carving out the gorge over five to six million years and exposing rocks that are up to two billion years old through vividly coloured strata. It's this incredible chromatic element that stays with you almost as much as the canyon's size, with the various layers of reds, ochres and yellows seemingly painted over the strangely shaped tower formations and broken cliffs. Think of it this way: the Grand Canyon is like a mountain range upside down. The country around the top is basically flat and all the rugged, craggy elements are below you. The abruptness of the drop is bizarre and for some, unnerving. But the Grand Canyon is like that: it picks you up and takes you out of your comfort zone, dropping you back just that little bit changed after all.

07
RAVELLING
secrets of Petra

t's easy to be overwhelmed by the architectural vonders of Petra, a city carved from stone on the edge of the Jordanian desert. Today, visitors enter hrough the most dramatic route possible, the narrow, curving passage through the sandstone jorge known as the Siq (the shaft); and as you approach you are afforded tantalising glimpses of he city's most iconic building, the Al Khazneh or Treasury, an elegant temple-like structure carved nto the face of the gorge. You might be familiar vith this – it was featured in the movie *Indiana Jones and the Last Crusade* – and in any case its classical acade has become the symbol of Petra and its ecrets. The city certainly has the latter, not least he mysterious people who built it, the Nabateans. Walk a little further, past the impressive theatre, and he valley opens out to form a plain hemmed in by hills and peach-coloured walls of rock. It's here that nost of their city once lay: ornate tombs cut into he rocks and ruined buildings dot the landscape.

No one knows much about the Nabateans – they eft us no writings and few inscriptions – and the city you see now is mostly the legacy of the Roman occupation of 106 AD. But what we do know is mpressive – like the fact that the Nabateans were accomplished engineers, manipulating flash floods o store enough water to maintain a constant upply, even in times of drought. Other evidence uggests the city was established between the ixth and fourth centuries BC, booming as a centre or the Arabian spice trade until a sixth-century earthquake destroyed its crucial water-saving echnology. It wasn't until 1812 that Petra was ediscovered by Swiss explorer Johann Ludwig Burckhardt, and excavations still continue, slowly adding to our understanding of this remarkable city's founders.

need to know

Petra is three hours south of Amman by coach (around JD12), and open daily: Oct–April 6.30am–5pm; May–Sept 6am–5.30pm. Entry is JD21 or JD25 or two days.

There's a point on the Inca Trail when you suddenly forget all the accumulated aches and pains of four days' hard slog across the Andes. You're standing at Inti Punku, the Sun Gate, the first golden rays of dawn slowly bringing the jungle to life. Down below, revealing itself in tantalizing glimpses as the early-morning mist burns gradually away, are the distinctive ruins of Machu Picchu, looking every bit the lost Inca citadel it was until less than a century ago.

Machu Picchu: the Road to Ruins

The hordes of visitors that will arrive by mid-morning are still tucked up in bed; for the next couple of hours or so, it's just you, your group and a small herd of llamas, grazing indifferently on the terraced Incan slopes. That first unforgettable sunrise view from Inti Punku is just the start: thanks to its remote location – hugging the peaks at 2500m and hidden in the mountains some 120km from Cusco – Machu Picchu escaped the ravages of the Spanish conquistadores and remained semi-buried in the Peruvian jungle until Hiram Bingham, an American explorer, "rediscovered" them in 1911. Which means that, descending onto the terraces and working your way through the stonework labrynth, you'll discover some of the best-preserved Incan remains in the world.

Sites such as the Temple of the Sun and the Intihuatana appear exactly as they did some six hundred years ago. The insight they give us into the cultures and customs of the Incas is still as rewarding – the former's window frames the constellation of Pleiades, an important symbol of crop fertitility – and their structural design, pieced together like an ancient architectural jigsaw, just as incredible.

need to know

Macchu Picchu is just three or four hours by train from Cusco, but it is far more rewarding to visit when incorporated as part of the Inca Trail. Hiking the trail can only be done on a tour or with a licensed guide; the number of trekkers is now limited to two hundred a day, so you should book your trip several months in advance. If flying straight into Cusco, allow at least three days to acclimatize to the altitude.

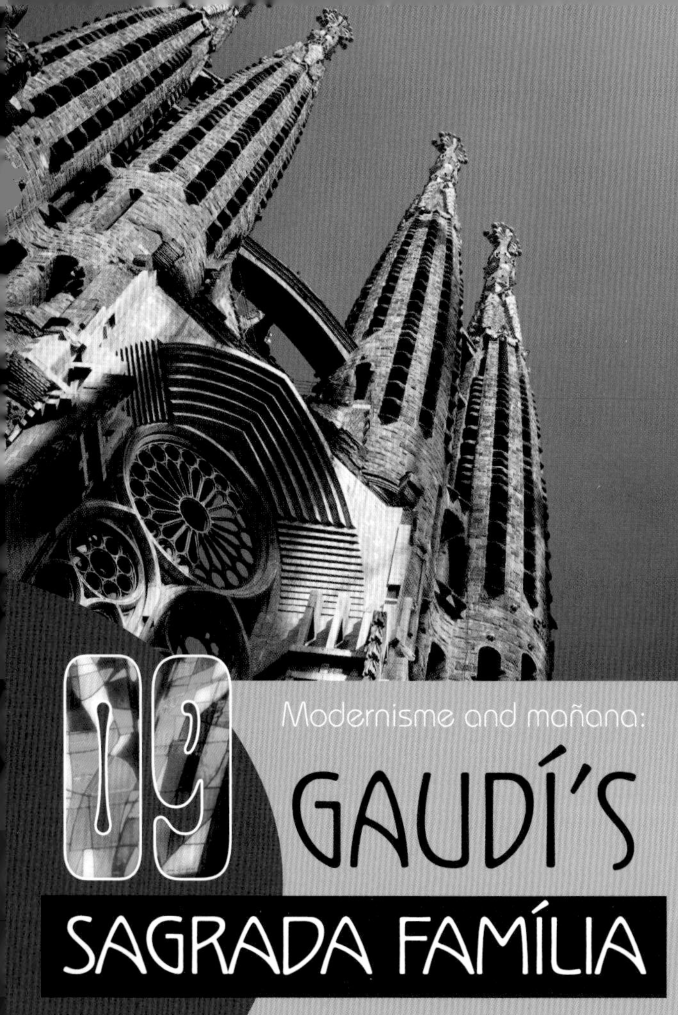

09 Modernisme and mañana: GAUDÍ'S SAGRADA FAMÍLIA

If you've ever been at the mercy of a Spanish tradesman, or merely tried to buy a litre of milk after midday, you'll know that the Iberian concept of time is not just slightly elastic but positively twangy. The master of twang, however, has to be Antoni Gaudí i Cornet, the Catalan architect whose *pièce de résistance* is famously still under construction more than a century after he took the project on: "My client is not in a hurry" was his jocular riposte to the epic timescale.

NEED TO KNOW **The Sagrada Família (daily April–Sept 9am–8pm; Oct–March 9am–6pm; €8) lies on the eastern edge of Barcelona's famous Eixample district. Nearby is La Pedrera, Gaudí's wave machine of an apartment block.**

Conceived as spiritual payback for secular radicalism, the Temple Expiatiori de la Sagrada Família consumed the final decade and a half of a life that had become increasingly reclusive. Gaudí couldn't have imagined that a new millennium would find his creation feted as a wonder of the post-modern world, symbolic of a Barcelona reborn and the single most popular tourist attraction in Spain. Craning your neck up to the totemic, honeycomb-gothic meltdown of the Sagrada Família's towers today, it's perhaps not so difficult to believe that he was a nature-loving vegetarian as well as an ardent Catholic and nationalist. By subsuming the organic intricacy of cellular life, his off-kilter *modernisme* wields a hypnotic, outlandish power, a complexity of design that entwines itself around your grey matter in a single glance. Which is half its charm; if you don't fancy dodging sweaty tourists and piles of mosaics in progress, simply take a constitutional around the exterior. Personally masterminded by Gaudí before his death, the Nativity facade garlands its virgin birth with microcosmic stone flora, a stark contrast to the Cubist austerity of the recently completed Passion façade.

The main reward for venturing inside is a squeamish elevator ride up one of the towers, a less tiring, crowded and claustrophobic experience than taking the stairs (hundreds of them!), leaving you with sufficient energy to goggle at the city through a prism of threaded stone and ceramics.

10

WALKING ON ICE

The Perito Moreno Glacier

FED BY ONE OF THE PLANET'S largest freshwater reserves – the Southern Patagonian Icecap – the Perito Moreno Glacier is the world's biggest ice-cube dispenser. It could also be described as a gigantic frozen Blue Lady, thanks to centuries of compression which has turned the deepest ice a deep shade of *curaçao*, whose sapphire veins can be tantalizingly glimpsed through plunging fissures. This icy leviathan of a cocktail is one to linger over, gradually letting it intoxicate you, as you survey its infiniteness from the viewing-platform across the Lago Argentino. One of the few advancing glaciers in the world, it does move, but, well, at glacial speed. It's noisy too, squeaking and whining and occasionally even exploding, as every few minutes a wardrobe-sized chunk splashes into the lake's chilly waters and bobs away as an iceberg. But the spectacular event you'll be hoping to see, the "ruptura", when Perito Moreno lunges forward, relatively speaking, forms a dam of ice and then violently breaks, only happens every four to five years. And throughout the 1990s it didn't happen at all…

A great way of getting to know this icy beast is to go for a walk on it. Standing on the glacier, you can see every crack and crevice, every tiny pinnacle. Even on a warm summer's day, the glacier, unsurprisingly, remains chilly, so wrap up well. Protect your eyes and exposed skin from the immense white glare with sunglasses and a high-factor sunscreen. The ice can be slippery but it's not dangerous, as long as you stick to sensible footwear and snap on the crampons issued by all the tour companies offering glacier-treks. They're a bit like soccer boots, but the spikes are adapted to snow and ice. And when you've walked far enough, you'll be glad to know that most treks end up with a tumbler of whisky on the rocks, made with ice-cubes chipped out of the glacier, of course.

need to know

The nearest town to the Perito Moreno Glacier is El Calafate, 80km away and a forty-hour bus ride or three-hour flight from Buenos Aires. The official website Ⓦwww.elcalafate.gov.ar is a mine of information on the glacier and how to visit. One of the best companies organizing mini-treks on the glacier is Hielo y Aventura, at Avenida del Libertador 935, El Calafate (Ⓣ02902/492094, Ⓦwww.hieloyaventura.com).

Doing Penance in the Sistine Chapel: Seeing Michelangelo's Frescoes

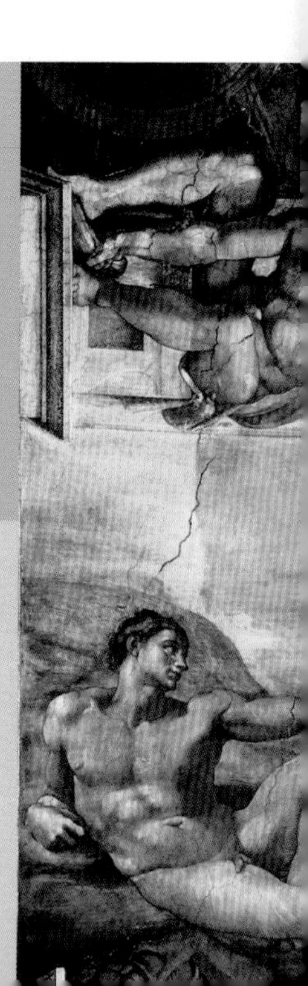

You've seen them a thousand times before you even get there. Michelangelo's ceiling and wall frescoes of the Sistine Chapel are perhaps the most recognizable pieces of art in the world, reproduced so much that they've become part of the visual furniture of our lives. Getting to this enormous work isn't easy; indeed, it's almost an act of penance in itself, waiting in endless queues and battling flag-following tour groups. But none of that, nor the simple entrance to the chapel, can prepare you for the magnificence of what lies beyond.

Despite the crowds, the noise and the periodic chiding of the guards, seeing these luminous paintings in the flesh for the first time is a moving experience. The ceiling frescoes get the most attention, although staring at them for long in the high barrel-vaulted chapel isn't great for the neck muscles. Commissioned by Pope Julius II in 1508, they depict scenes from the Old Testament, from the *Creation of Light* at the altar end to the *Drunkenness of Noah* at the other, interspersed with pagan sybils and biblical prophets, who peer out spookily from between the vivid main scenes. Look out for the hag-like *Cumean sybil,* and the prophet *Jeremiah*, a self-portrait of an exhausted-looking Michelangelo. Or just gaze in wonder at the whole decorative scheme – not bad for someone who considered himself a sculptor rather than a painter.

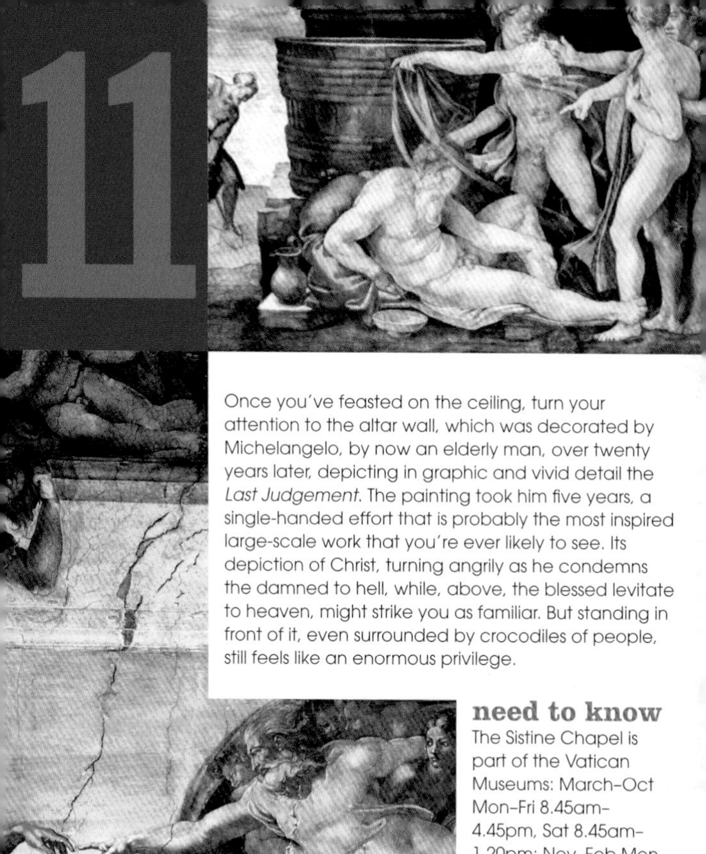

Once you've feasted on the ceiling, turn your attention to the altar wall, which was decorated by Michelangelo, by now an elderly man, over twenty years later, depicting in graphic and vivid detail the *Last Judgement*. The painting took him five years, a single-handed effort that is probably the most inspired large-scale work that you're ever likely to see. Its depiction of Christ, turning angrily as he condemns the damned to hell, while, above, the blessed levitate to heaven, might strike you as familiar. But standing in front of it, even surrounded by crocodiles of people, still feels like an enormous privilege.

need to know

The Sistine Chapel is part of the Vatican Museums: March–Oct Mon–Fri 8.45am–4.45pm, Sat 8.45am–1.20pm; Nov–Feb Mon–Sat 8.45am–12.20pm; closed Sun, except the last Sun of each month, when it's free – one of the world's great travel bargains.

12 Sacred peaks

trekking in the Himalayas

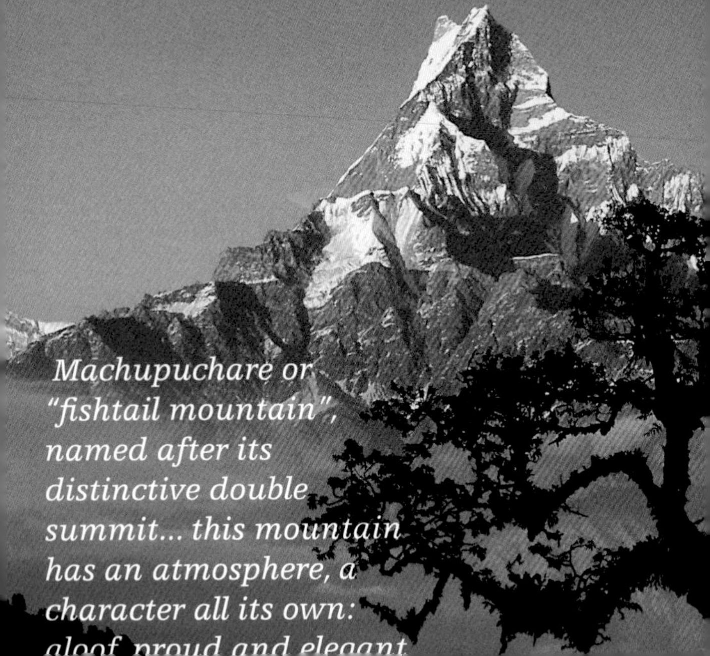

Machupuchare or "fishtail mountain", named after its distinctive double summit... this mountain has an atmosphere, a character all its own: aloof, proud and elegant

Seeing the Himalayas from the air feels almost voyeuristic, as if you're cheating by being at the same altitude. However, I couldn't resist pressing my nose against the window as we began our descent to Kathmandu, an amber glow radiating from the snowy peaks above the valley as the sky turned from black to purple, then blue. It was October and the monsoon clouds had cleared – perfect trekking time.

A week later I was heading into the foothills of the spectacular Annapurna range with Jhamka and Baburam, my guide and porter. I'd considered going it alone, but, as each day passed, I was increasingly glad of their companionship, learning Nepali songs and the names of plants and animals we encountered along the way – everything from marijuana to macaques. As we moved from low-level bamboo forest to the steeper trails, I caught my first glimpse of Machupuchare or 'Fishtail Mountain', named after its distinctive double summit. Just shy of 7000m, it's an altitudinal also-ran by the warped standards of Nepal, but has an atmosphere all of its own – even from this distance, with a classic pyramidal shape that ticks every box. Aloof, proud and elegant, it's revered by Hindus, and off-limits to climbers.

The cool air began to thin as we continued into the 'sanctuary', a natural ampitheatre carved out by a long-departed glacier and home to Annapurna Base Camp (a mere 4130m up). Early the next morning, as the sun inched over the black ridge above us, we witnessed the gradual illumination of Annapurna – at 8091m, a legend among climbers in that it was the first eight-thousand-metre peak to be conquered. Finally putting away my camera, a sad realization dawned – it was time to head back down to Earth.

need to know

Nepal's main trekking season runs from late September to late November, when the skies are clear and the weather pleasantly warm, even at high altitude. Given the unpredictable security situation, trekking alone is not recommended and you will get a lot more out of your trip with an experienced guide. You should seek consular advice if planning on travelling outside the main trekking areas of Annapurna, Everest and north of Kathmandu.

18

DEEP IN THE JUNGLE

The amazing temples of

ANGKOR WAT

The sun was setting on the town of Siem Reap as I clung to the back of my moto driver. Threading our way through traffic, we rode out until town finally gave way to forest and we entered the Angkor site. In front of us were the iconic lotus-bud towers of Angkor Wat, looking like giant pine cones, resplendent in the light. Sunset is the best time to view west-facing Angkor Wat, from the top of nearby temple-mountain, Phnom Bakheng, when the greying stone of the towers glow red under the glare of the dying sun.

The secret of Angkor is to explore the galleries and enclosures at your own pace. Wander the corridors and you'll stumble across aged monks performing blessings on curious tourists; wafting bundles of burning incense over their body and loudly clapping a cupped palm across their back. The outer walls of the temple are covered with bas-reliefs retelling stories of Hindu battles and mythology, whose intricately etched bodies are worn smooth by the fingers of thousands of hands. And all around is the echo of children playing in the cool passageways and juvenile hawkers who sell cold drinks and trinkets out of plastic carrier bags.

The next morning I went back to see Angkor Thom, with its lichen covered towers of the Bayon revealing exquisite faces carved into rock. Fat, curvaceous lips smiling benevolently beneath half-closed eyes. Thick jungle once shrouded this lost twelfth-century Khmer kingdom: the site of which is amazing. Its painstaking restoration involved numbering and cataloguing each stone block before setting it back into its original position. The destructive force of nature and time on stone is no more evident than at Ta Prohm, the temple left to the jungle. Here huge tree trunks, hard as cement, spill out over the scattered blocks like the creamy bellies of snakes. It's a wonderfully peaceful place, and once you're done exploring the doorways and curious shapes of the forest over boulder, sit back, kick off your shoes and listen to the noise of insects whirring in the sun and birds squawking in a soothing blend of background noise.

need to know

To visit the Angkor complex you need a pass valid for one day ($20), three days ($40) or seven days ($60). Most popular is the three-day pass. The Angkor site is around 5km away from Siem Reap; there are plenty of motorbike taxis to transport you to the site and between temples, or you can hire a bike. Regular flights service Siem Reap from Bangkok and Phnom Penh, or catch a boat from Phnom Penh.

In Venice you are constantly coming upon something that amazes: a magnificent and dilapidated palace, a lurching church tower, an impossibly narrow alleyway that ends in the water. The coffee-table books don't lie – this really is the most beautiful city in the world. The thing is, it's so beautiful that you might not see just how remarkable it is.

Weaving your way through the city, you have to remind yourself that every single building is a miracle of ingenuity: the urban fabric of Venice is extraordinarily dense, but the walls have been raised on nothing more than mudflats. The canalscapes are picturesque, undeniably, but they're an extremely efficient circulatory system as well – freight in Venice goes by water, leaving pedestrians in complete control of the land. Venice was also a pioneer of industrial technologies: the glass factories of Murano were one of the continent's earliest manufacturing zones, while the dockyards of the Arsenale were Europe's first production line, operating so smoothly that a functioning battleship could be assembled in the course of a day. Socially and politically, too, Venice was in the vanguard. At a time when most other European states were ruled by monarchs and hoodlums, Venice was a republic, and it lasted for a thousand years.

At its zenith, Venice was a metropolis of some 200,000 people (about three times the present population), with an empire that extended from the Dolomites to Cyprus, and trading networks that spread right across Asia. And trade was what made this one of Europe's great multicultural cities: the main post office was once the HQ of the German merchants; the natural history museum occupies the premises of the Turkish traders; and all over the city you'll find traces of its Greek, Albanian, Slavic, Armenian and Jewish communities.

Of course, the monuments of Venice attract tourists in their millions. Most, however, see nothing more than St Mark's Square. To escape the crowds, and see the place clearly, you just have to stroll for ten minutes in any direction and lose yourself in the world's most remarkable labyrinth.

need to know

Venice's tourist season is virtually an all-year affair, so book your room well in advance. The tourist office's website (Ⓦwww.turismovenezia.it) gives details of accommodation of all types, while the Venetian Hoteliers' Association (Ⓦwww.veneziasi.it) lists hundreds of hotels.

14

Venice: Europe's first modern city?

15 The Sahara

Getting back to basics with the people of the veil

need to know

Tour agencies in Agadez can organize camel treks from around €60 a day. Charter flights run to Agadez from Paris between October and April (price

The Sahara is the world's largest hot desert – and arguably the most desolate, inhospitable place on earth. It's roughly the size of the USA, yet has a population of less than a million people, and its vast expanse divides North Africa from so-called sub-Saharan Africa in a great swathe of dunes, sand seas, mountains and plateaus.

How do you get to experience this natural wonder? Well, not surprisingly the traditional caravan routes in Northern Africa have long since been supplanted by more modern modes of transport. But a camel journey across the Sahara is not just a retro-chic way of 'doing the desert', it adds up to an authentic and intimate experience that gets to the core of the desert's appeal. You become immersed in the landscape at a natural pace, savouring the simplicity, space and silence.

Your journey begins a day's drive from Agadez in northern Niger. Camels grumble as loads are lashed to their backs, but saddles are mostly unoccupied. Forget the romantic image of the dromedary's lolling gait transporting you effortlessly over the sands. A camel is more mule than horse so you'll be on foot most of the time. Your Tuareg guide will show you how to put on the traditional turban or *tagelmoust* worn by all desert men, and soon you'll adapt to their pace, rising at dawn, strolling towards a shady noontime rest, and camping again around mid-afternoon when the camels are unloaded to forage for food. You cover around 15km a day, stopping along the way for mint tea at scruffy encampments where half-naked kids chase the goats and girls giggle shyly from behind their indigo shawls. The landscape is more diverse than you might expect, with the 2000-metre-high blue-grey peaks of Niger's Aïr Mountains merging with the amber-pink sand sheet of the Ténéré Desert far beyond the eastern horizon – the classic Saharan combination.

Tuareg nomad culture is alive and well in the Aïr despite a hostile government in the distant capital, Niamey. But 'Tuareg' is in fact a derogatory Arabic term. From southwest Libya to Timbuktu in Mali these proud nomads describe themselves collectively as Kel Tagelmoust: "the People of the Veil".

"If you've never been to the Great Wall, you're not a real man."

So said Mao Zedong, the anti-Imperialist leader who was bowled over by China's grandest Imperial legacy.

Ever since it was claimed that the Great Wall of China was the only man-made structure visible from space (generally considered untrue), it's been hard to divorce legend from reality when it comes to describing one of the world's great feats of engineering. After all, the Wall does have truly extraordinary proportions. No one knows the exact length, but 4800km is a conservative estimate, stretching from Shanhaiguan on the Yellow Sea to the deserts of Xinjiang; and with a history of over 2000 years, it's hard to remain unimpressed even by the statistics.

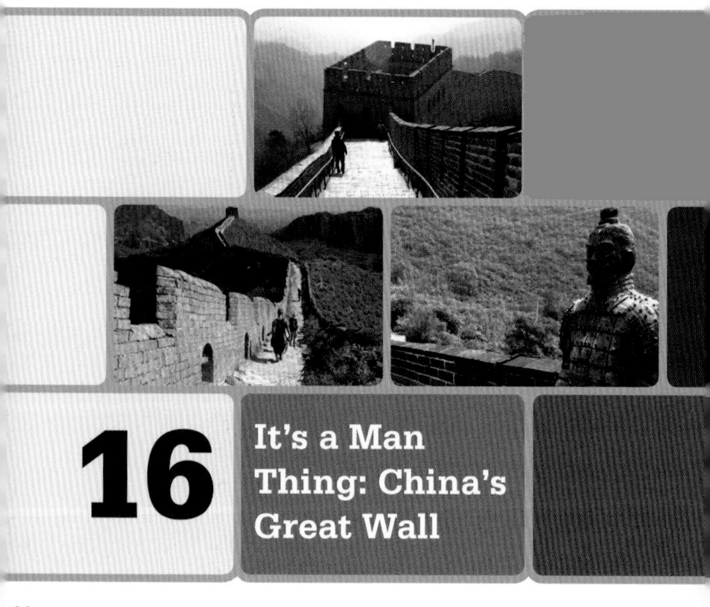

16 It's a Man Thing: China's Great Wall

The truth is that the 'Great Wall' is an amalgam of several structures, built over many centuries; in fact it's almost impossible to trace the wall in a continuous line. The solid Ming dynasty version that most tourists see today, built in the sixteenth century, was essentially useless – when the Manchu army invaded in 1644 they convinced a Ming general to open the gates, and it's been redundant ever since.

So why all the hype? Well, the wall is hauntingly beautiful, especially at dawn or sunset, and in the spring when the hills around Beijing are laden with peach blossom. But it's the sheer audacity of the project, and the technical proficiency required to achieve it, that beggars belief. The route it follows is utterly astounding, if not insane, literally taking the hardest, steepest, most preciptious line across the hills, in total disregard for the laws of physics. In some places it's like climbing a stone ladder. All in all it's a staggering symbol of the absolute power of the Chinese emperors, and the exceptional skills of the people of the time – and as such is an experience not to be missed.

need to know

Many sections of the Great Wall are accessible as day-trips from Beijing: regular tourist buses run to Badaling (daily 9am–4.30pm; ¥35), Mutianyu (daily 8am–4pm; ¥35) and Simatai (daily 8am–4pm; ¥32).

17 THE SMOKE THAT THUNDERS at Victoria Falls

You know that a place is special when it can inspire true love. Victoria Falls is just such a spot. Over 500 million litres of water crashing every minute from heights of up to 450 metres is a pretty powerful phenomenon; it creates an intangible but nonetheless potent magic in the air. Looking around, you'll see it in the eyes of vacationing couples, or in that young pair who have met on their travels, now locked together, a fine spray of warm mist shrouding them as they succumb to the irresistible power of the Falls' charms.

And for the non-romantics? Well, there's plenty to do other than gaze into someone's eyes. Vic Falls is a huge draw for adventure sport addicts – the mighty Zambezi river, from which the Falls flow, offers up white-water rafting that is widely thought to be second-to-none. Or you could try plunging by bungy 110m from the bridge between Zambia and Zimbabwe – the roar of the falls, and likely your screams, ringing in your ears. For a different perspective, book a hot air balloon, microlight or helicopter ride and marvel at the bird's-eye view of what the locals call Mosi-oa-Tunya – 'The Smoke That Thunders'.

High-octane madness aside, your experience would be equally as spectacular just ambling along the network of marked paths in the surrounding rainforest, sharing the trail with a baboon or two before the lush, dense foliage opens up to vistas of the world's most incredible curtain of ever-flowing water.

Is that a twinkle in your eye?

need to know

Victoria Falls lie on the border of Zimbabwe, in its northwestern corner, with Zambia to the north. Both sides of the border offer views of the Falls: ideally you would get to experience both sides but due to political difficulties in Zimbabwe, Livingstone in Zambia is the base of choice for most travellers, and it's here you can book adventure activities. The best time to visit is between April and June when the river is in flood.

The Caribbean coastline of Belize is something of a paradise cliché. The second-largest coral reef in the world, all 320km of it, runs the length of the country, sheltering around 1200 small islands, or "cayes", in its calm inshore waters – some are developed tourist resorts, others low-key backpacker haunts and uninhabited palm-shaded sandbanks. As if this wasn't enough, three of the Caribbean's four coral atolls (extinct volcanoes) are close offshore, providing stupendous diving. Cliché, indeed.

The Blue Hole may be the most famous of these atolls, but the best developed is Glover's Reef. About 50km off Dangriga, it spans 35km from north to south, and is encircled by deep, stunning walls of coral. A handful of cayes pepper the central lagoon; underwater, they're surrounded by several hundred colourful patch reefs.

To explore Glover's by sea kayak couldn't be more perfect. The cayes in the central lagoon are a good place to start out – each has a white-coral beach, and all are easy to reach. Many visitors elect to go as part of a guided tour, but it's also possible to spend a few days on your own, meandering from caye to caye, camping and living on barbecued grouper and lobster. More adventurous kayakers can head miles out to sea through calm swells, where, although you leave your human companions behind, you're never alone – pelicans, nesting ospreys and other sea birds are always close by. Snorkelling straight off the kayak reveals staggering underwater biodiversity – sea turtles, parrotfish, rays and dolphins all make frequent appearances, and whale sharks haunt the waters around Glover's in the spring. If laid-back Belize really has really got under your skin, opt for a kayak with a kite sail, which allows you to sit back and follow the trade winds through the cayes. Bliss.

PADDLING BELIZE'S BARRIER REEF 18

need to know Boats from Sittee River and Dangriga travel to the reef at least once a week; each caye within Glover's central lagoon has a dive operator that organizes tours or rents equipment.

19
Romancing the *Taj*

"It's a majestic and humbling experience, and hard to take in on a first visit."

It's almost with a sense of duty, rather than excitement, that you approach Agra and the Taj Mahal. In fact, the rest of the country is such an assault on the senses that you might find it difficult to muster up the energy to do even this. Then again you may just find this elegant symbol of love the perfect antidote.

The Moghul emperor Shah Jahan built the Taj Mahal for his beloved wife, Mumtaz Mahal, after her death in 1631; and whichever angle you look at it from, it is an undeniably impressive building. Arriving through the matted tangle of Agra's dusty streets, your first real glimpse will be the classic one: the cream-coloured core, flanked by four elegant minarets and crowned by the voluptuous dome and its diminutive cupolas. Approaching through the manicured gardens, the exquisite details of the inscriptions carved into the face of the marble slowly come into focus. While ascending the steps into the heart of the tomb, your eyes are automatically drawn up into the seemingly infinite depth of the inner dome, while your bare feet are soothed by the cool floor. It's a majestic and humbling experience, and hard to take in on a first visit.

Above all the Taj is a monument to love, but this only really registers when you gaze back at the building from Agra Fort, across the bend in the Yamuna River. It was here that Shah Jahan died after being incarcerated by his son Aurangzeb; and here too, looking longingly across to the Taj from an arched sandstone window, that he pined daily for his lost love.

need to know

Agra is 204km southeast of the capital New Delhi. There are four flights, over twenty trains, and numerous buses daily between the two cities, as well as many tour buses. Accommodation to suit all budgets is easily available. Entrance to the Taj Mahal is now a steep 750 rupees (nearly £9/$17), unlike the 50 paise (half a rupee) I paid in 1989.

MAYA RUINS: Live Museums to a Lost Civilization

20

THE RUINS OF FAILED civilizations exude a dark power, and nowhere is this more true than the great Maya sites of Mexico and Guatemala. The most excavated, and consequently best-known, are Palenque in Chiapas, Uxmal in the Yucatán, both in Mexico, along with Tikal's soaring vertical pyramids in Guatemala's Petén jungle; and other cities of this complex and sophisticated civilization are still being excavated – Bonampak, Chaccoben, Chac Mool. Each one has something different to offer: Palenque is complex and varied architecturally; Tikal is most impressive for the sheer height of its pyramids; Bonampak's murals depict the sacred and everyday lives of the Maya.

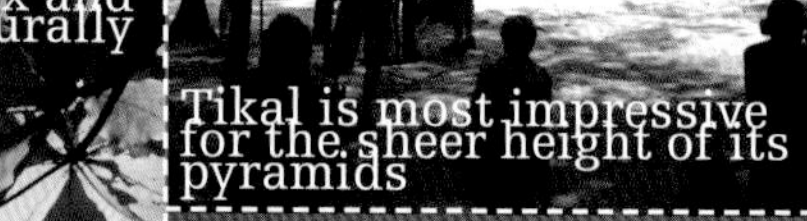

Tikal is most impressive for the sheer height of its pyramids

Palenque is complex and varied architecturally

First glances of these great cities are always memorable: immense pyramids soar above dense jungle, like wrecked ocean liners of a forgotten age. Wandering across the empty plazas of these former cities, it is impossible not to meditate on the downfall of the Maya – whose primary cause, most experts now agree, was due to a collapse in their agricultural system, combined with overpopulation. Scramble to the top of the Temple of the Inscriptions at Palenque, and you can descend amid the must and gloom to a centuries-old vault where a precious turquoise mask has been unearthed. The views are awe-inspiring: from the Temple of the Inscriptions at Palenque you can see the tangled scrub of the Yucatán peninsula for a hundred miles; and each of the five temples at Tikal offers a heady, vertigo-inducing view of dense rainforest – and at dusk you may see macaws zinging between the branches of the surrounding Ceiba trees.

There is a mystical element to these heat-shimmered ex-metropolises which is somehow manages not to be eroded by the visitor's centres, the tourist buses and souvenir stalls. They are live museums, unique in their grandeur and the beauty of their setting, to a vanished civilization.

Bonampak's murals depict the sacred and everyday lives of the Maya

need to know

The town of **Palenque** is reachable by regular bus from Mérida – a nine-hour journey – or from Mexico City (17 hours). The ruins are just outside the town and reachable by regular buses. **Bonampak** can be visited on a day-trip from Palenque; it's three hours by bus to San Javier and then a short taxi ride. There are lots of buses to **Uxmal** from Mérida, and the journey takes about two hours. **Tikal** is easily reachable by bus from the nearby towns of Santa Elena and Flores, or by bus direct rom Guatemela City airport.

The Giants of Rapa Nui

21

An insignificant speck in the South Pacific, Easter Island, or Rapa Nui in Polynesian, is one of the most isolated islands in the world. South America lies 3600km to the east, and with the vast expanse of the Pacific never far from view, the sense of utter isolation can be unnerving. Yet despite its location, Easter Island is famous thanks to the enigmatic *moai*, whose squat torsos and long, brooding heads loom sombrely over the island's coastline, their mysterious existence making them symbols of lost civilization, crackpot Atlantis theories, alien intelligence, or, more plausibly, ecological disaster.

The *moai* might look familiar, but it's only when you visit the island that the overwhelming scale of their construction sinks in – it's littered with hundreds of them, most toppled over, face down in the tussock grass. The carvings, many 30m tall, have a majestic, serene quality that is certainly captivating, and it

helps that many have been raised and restored, top knots and coral eyes included. Thought to represent the ancestors of the Polynesian tribe that settled on the island some time before the eleventh century, it's easy to see why their obsessive production intensified the drift towards catastrophe. No one knows why the carvers dropped their tools and abandoned their work so suddenly. Or what caused this highly organized society to self-destruct, descending into anarchy, but by the time the first European ships arrived here in the eighteenth century, only a few impoverished villages remained. Today, the sleepy settlement of Hanga Roa exists only for tourists and virtually every morsel of food is imported on weekly flights from Chile.

So how did the Polynesians even find this place, never mind survive? The longer you stay, the more impossible it seems that people travelling thousands of miles in canoes could ever get here. By the time you leave, Easter Island's secrets will seem more unfathomable than ever, and those theories of alien intervention and lost Atlantis less cranky after all.

need to know

Lan Chile (Ⓦwww.lan.com) makes the five-hour flight to Easter Island three times a week from Santiago. Round-trip fares start at around US$670.

22
Sacred Space: The Grand Mosque in Djenné

Mali is a treasure box of a country, where fishermen ply the River Niger in brightly-painted pirogues, kora-playing *jalis* sing songs written for the rulers of an ancient, glittering empire and the faithful worship in spectacular mosques made of timber and mud.

Djenné's Grande Mosquée is the most famous of all. Beautifully simple but with a potent presence, it exudes the kind of gravitas shared by all the world's great sacred buildings. But there's also something gloriously organic – sensuous, even – about its Soudanic curves and crenellations; and it's a fitting focal point for a community which guards its traditions fiercely while embracing a brand of Islam that is neither repressive nor restrictive. Djenné itself is seeped in history, and works hard to maintain its meticulously preserved state. Mud-built houses need regular attention, and at the end of each rainy season the whole town pitches in to make good the russet facades. Several hundred workers scale the walls of the Grande Mosquée with the help of the timber struts that sprout from the minarets like bristles.

Visit the Grande Mosquée on any Monday and it's abuzz with activity of a different sort. In the large, dusty marketplace in front of the mosque, traders preside over pyramids of knobbly bitter tomatoes or sacks of pungent dried fish, Fula women with heavy gold earrings pore over brightly patterned cotton fabrics and rickety donkey carts weave through the crowds. The market is thoroughly absorbing. But to appreciate Djenné more deeply, you'll need to stay on after the hubbub has dispersed, and savour that last, golden hour of the day when the call of the muezzin wafts over the city, just as it has every evening for seven hundred years.

need to know

Djenné is 30km from the main road between the Malian capital, Bamako, and the junction town of Mopti; bush taxis run from Mopti to Djenné, most frequently on market days. The interior of the mosque is open to Muslims only.

MIGHTY REAL IN *Las Vegas*

23

New York City has its skyscrapers, Cairo the pyramids, Paris the Eiffel Tower, Venice its canals. Las Vegas? It's got all the above, and then some.

People travel round the globe in search of the authentic. But you won't find this in Vegas. In their place are simulacra, kitschy homage and pure, unadulterated spectacle. Here the hotel entrepreneurs play an ever-higher-stakes game of "Can you top this?", and everything has to be newer, bigger, and brighter than before. In fact, the newness of everything is a fake, too. What's new really means what's been done before and re-imagined. The Forum Shops at *Caesars Palace*? A cunningly themed shopping mall that's an indoor re-creation of Rome's open-air bazaar, where the 'sky' (well, the ceiling) changes as the day goes on. Nobu Matsuhisa's inviting namesake restaurant in the *Hard Rock Hotel*? A splashier replica of his original, internationally acclaimed raw-fish emporium in Manhattan. It's no wonder that so much of the big-ticket night-time entertainment is centred around magicians and gravity-defying acts like Cirque du Soleil. The whole of Las Vegas is an illusion, and one that to most people is utterly irresistible – and, just as importantly, unabashedly, trashily American. Who needs the whiff of authenticity when you've got all this in one place? The smoky glass pyramid of the *Luxor*, from which emanates the world's most powerful beam of light, is heralded by an enormous sphinx. The choreographed fountains at the giant lake in front of the *Bellagio* can't help but thrill. You can ride on a gondola at *The Venetian* – inside the hotel – or a rollercoaster at *New York-New York*. And most importantly you can sustain the illusion for as long as you want – or can afford it. No wonder no one ever wants to leave.

need to know

Las Vegas is in the middle of the desert in Nevada; plenty of flights go there daily from across the world. The Strip, a four-mile stretch of hotel-casinos along Las Vegas Boulevard (eight of the ten largest hotels in the world call Vegas home), is the city's beating heart.

A GILDED CAGE: Exploring the Forbidden City

The Gugong, or Imperial Palace, is much better known in the West by its unofficial title, the Forbidden City, a reference to the fact that for five centuries, through the reigns of 24 emperors of the Ming and Qing dynasties, ordinary Chinese people were forbidden from even approaching its walls. This giant complex of eight hundred buildings and nine thousand chambers was the symbolic centre of the Chinese universe. From within the 'Sons of Heaven', ruled the Empire in a private realm of pomp and pageantry, served by enormous retinues of concubines and eunuchs, and few ventured outside unless they had to. It remains an extraordinary place today, unsurpassed in China – or, perhaps, anywhere – for its monumental scale, harmonious design and elegant grandeur.

The plan of the palace buildings is essentially Ming, with most buildings dating back to the fifteenth century. Construction involved up to ten thousand artisans and perhaps a million labourers. Roads were iced over to move the huge marble blocks and enormous trees had to be floated on canals all the way from Southern China.

The halls are laid out according to geomantic theories. The buildings face south in order to benefit from the invigorating yang energy, and as a protection against harmful yin elements from the north, both real and imagined – cold winds, evil spirits and steppe barbarians. Ramparts and a fifty-metre-wide moat isolated the complex from the commoners outside, with the only access being through monumental gateways in the four cardinal directions. The layout is the same as any grand Chinese house of the period; pavilions are arranged around courtyards, with reception rooms and official buildings at the front (south), arranged with rigorous symmetry, and a labyrinth of private chambers to the north. The central halls are the most magnificent, but for many visitors it's the side rooms, with their displays of the intimate accoutrements of court life – the decorative flywhisks and uncomfortable thrones, the endlessly repeated motifs of dragons and phoenixes, the high shine of lacquer and sparkle of precious metals, the stiff formality of the gorgeous clothes – that bring home the realities of life for the inhabitants of this, the most gilded of cages.

need to know

24

The Forbidden City is at the heart of Beijing, the Chinese capital, and is open daily 8.30am–5pm in summer, 8.30am–4.30pm in winter. Tickets are ¥40; the ¥60 ticket includes entry to a couple of special exhibitions. The easiest way to get there is to take the metro to Tian'anmen West or Tian'anmen East.

25 Itaipú: plugging the world's biggest dam

Colossal, gargantuan, mammoth, gigantic

– it's difficult to find the right adjective to capture the sheer magnitude of the Itaipú dam. The joint property of Paraguay and Brazil, it has been voted one of the seven wonders of the modern world by the American society of civil engineers (who, I guess, should know what they're talking about), and is arguably man's greatest ever feat of practical engineering, virtually meeting the energy needs of the whole of Paraguay as well as a large chunk of southern Brazil. You don't need to be mechanically-minded to appreciate it either: the introductory video about the finer details of electricity generation might not hold your attention, but the sheer, awe-inspiring scale of the structure certainly will.

It took sixteen years to build the dam, a project that was begun in the dark days of Stroessner's dictatorship and reached its completion in the early years of democracy; its inception created a reservoir so deep and wide that it completely flooded the Sete Quedas, a set of waterfalls comparable in size to those at nearby Iguazú. At 8km long

and 195m high, standing next to it and looking up is as dizzying as you might expect. But to really feel insignificant, make a visit to the inside of the dam and the extraordinary one-kilometre-long machine room. Like the inside of an anthill, workers scurry around, dwarfed by the sheer scale of their surroundings. The dam is at its most impressive when water levels are at their peak, which could be at any time of year but is more likely to be during the rainy season, when torrents of water rush down the chutes and the roar can be deafening. Whenever you're here, though, it's an amazing sight – and one that for once does justice to even the highest expectations.

need to know

The visitor's centre for the Paraguayan side of the Itaipú dam is about 20km north of Ciudad del Este along the Supercarretera Itaipú. Visits are by guided tour only (Mon–Fri 9.30am, 1.30pm & 3pm, Sat 9.30am; free) and you'll need your passport to gain entry.

TC-BRP
KAPADOKYABALLOONS.COM

Ultimate experiences Wonders of the World miscellany

1 People

The world's **oldest** living person was Jeanne Louise Calment who died in France in 1997 at an astounding 122 years old. The only thing that is perhaps more remarkable is the net worth of the world's **richest** man, Bill Gates, estimated at US$53bn by Forbes (2006) and larger than the GDPs of Morocco, Vietnam and many other moderately sized nations. The total number of **billionaires** in the world is 793.

2 India

India is one of the world's oldest civilizations, home to numerous wonders, a vast culinary tradition, an incredibly eclectic blend of cultures and over one billion people. But what makes it truly astonishing is its status as the **world's largest democracy**: India has held democratic elections since 1950.

3 Shopping

On completion in 2008, the Dubai Mall in the United Arab Emirates is expected to be the world's largest shopping mall, with a total area of 1.115 million square metres (or over 100 football pitches) and containing an aquarium, ice rink and gold market.

Until then, you'll have to make do with the West Edmonton Mall, just outside Edmonton, Canada, or the only slightly more diminutive Mall of America, on the outskirts of Minneapolis, USA.

"The world will never starve for want of wonders; but only for want of wonder."

G.K. Chesterton

4 Wonders of the Stone Age

Cave art: Prehistoric cave art in France dates back 30,000 years, often vivid depictions of animals in caves such Grotte de Lascaux and Chauvet-Pont d'Arc, though Australia contains many Aboriginal art sites dating back almost as far.

Ice man: The startlingly well-preserved body of Ötzi, the "ice man" frozen in the Alps around 5300 BC and displayed in Bolzano (Italy), offers an incredible insight into the sophistication of Neolithic civilization - what they ate, the clothes they wore, and how they lived and died.

Music: The 8000-year-old bone flute displayed in the Henan Provincial Museum, Zhengzhou, China, is thought to be the oldest musical instrument ever found.

Stone circles: Stonehenge in the UK is perhaps the most famous stone circle, built around 3100 BC, although Carnac in France has the world's largest ensemble of standing stones, dating back to about 3300 BC.

Venus of Willendorf: Over 22,000 years old and one of numerous plump "Venus" figurines found in Europe, perhaps a symbol of fertility or an image of the Earth Mother. She's in the collection of Vienna's natural history museum.

5 Books

It's long been accepted that the **Bible** is the world's best-selling book with an estimated 5-6 billion copies sold, but it's now thought that the **Harry Potter** series by British writer J.K. Rowling is the most popular fiction ever created, with almost one billion books sold worldwide. Rowling is thought to have a net worth of around US$1billion.

The world's largest **library** is the Library of Congress in Washington DC, with over 29 million books, a little way ahead of London's British Library, which has about 25 million volumes.

6 Food and drink

Almost every culture on the planet has culinary dishes that outsiders find repulsive. The Cantonese are renowned for eating anything with its "back to the sky" – as well as the relatively prosaic stewed dog and cat, dehydrated tiger testicles and monkey brains occasionally grace menus. In Cambodia it's possible to eat tarantula spiders, maggot-like witchety grubs in Australia, calf's head in France and seal flippers in Newfoundland.

▸▸ Restaurants

According to Forbes, *Aragawa*, in Tokyo, rates as the world's most expensive restaurant, with average meals going for around US$300 per head.

▸▸ Drinks

According to the WHO, the most **alcoholic nations** (measured by alcohol units consumed per capita) are: Czech Republic and Ireland (beer); Luxembourg and France (wine); Moldova and Russia (spirits, namely vodka). Moldova is the overall leader, with almost 11 litres of alcohol consumed per person annually.

The most expensive **cocktail** is reputed to be the Ritz Side Car served at the Hemingway Bar, Paris Ritz, while the most expensive **wine** ever sold was a bottle of 1787 Chateau Lafite for £105,000.

The most expensive **coffee** is the infamous Kopi Luwak at US$300 per pound (0.45kg). The coffee is made from the excrement of civet cats in Irian Jaya, Indonesia, who live off the ripest coffee beans.

The record for the world's strongest **beer** is held by Sam Adam's Utopias, which is 25% alcohol and regularly released in limited editions of 3000 bottles every few years. It's also the world's most expensive beer at $100 a bottle. Among more affordable brews, the strongest beers are Samichlaus, produced each year in Austria for Christmas (14%); Aventus Weizen-Eisbock – 13%; and the Belgian Trappist ale Westvleteren, which weighs in at around 12%.

7 Hotels

The world's most peculiar hotel is perhaps Sweden's **IceHotel**, located in the village of Jukkasjärvi, 200km north of the Arctic Circle, made entirely from blocks of ice every year: guests sleep in thermal sleeping bags in rooms featuring ice beds and furniture.

The **Emirates Palace** in Abu Dhabi is the most lavish and expensive hotel ever built (US$2bn) and its lobby features the largest dome in the world, at 60m high. Palace suites cost around £8000 per night.

8 The natural world

The Serengeti **migration** in East Africa is perhaps the single greatest spectacle in the animal kingdom, involving 1.5 million buffalo, gazelles, wildebeest and zebra moving north to south through Kenya and Tanzania in October, and back again in April.

The world's **tallest tree**, discovered in September 2006, is Hyperion, a redwood in northern California. At 115.5m it's taller than St Paul's Cathedral in London.

"Let both sides seek to invoke the wonders of science instead of its terrors."

John F. Kennedy

▸▸ Aral Sea

Despite some improvements in the last two years, the Aral Sea in Central Asia is surely the world's largest man-made disaster: a once vast natural lake, it has not only been heavily polluted from weapons testing and industry, but it has also been reduced in size by 60% over the last forty years (mainly as a result of river diversion), and whole villages and fleets of ships lie stranded in the sand, hundreds of miles from water.

9 Seven amazing festivals

Germany: The Oktoberfest in Munich is the world's biggest beer festival, attracting over seven million visitors annually.

India: Held every 12 years, the sacred Hindu festival of Kumbh Mela was attended by 20 million people in 1995.

Philippines: Every Easter bloody re-enactments of the Crucifixion (where participants are actually nailed to crosses) take place in Pampanga province.

Spain: In Buñol every August over 25,000 people take part in the juice-soaked *La Tomatina*, bombarding each other with tomatoes.

Taiwan: The town of Yanshuei celebrates the Chinese Lantern Festival in February with thousands of "Beehive Fireworks", fired horizontally straight into the crowds.

Trinidad: A huge joyful, rum-soaked celebration, Trinidad's carnival is by far the biggest in the Caribbean.

USA: September's Burning Man is not the oldest, and definitely not the most traditional, but it's surely the weirdest large-scale annual event of them all.

10 Theme parks

Disney World

The world's first themed amusement park, Disneyland, opened in California in 1955. Today the Walt Disney World Resort in Orlando, Florida, covers 46 square miles and is the largest and most popular theme park in the world, comprising the Magic Kingdom, the Epcot Centre, Disney-MGM Studios and the Animal Kingdom: 16.2 million people visited the Magic Kingdom alone in 2005.

Rollercoasters

The longest rollercoaster in the world is the Steel Dragon 2000 at Nagashima Spa Land in Japan at 2479m. The tallest (127.4m) and fastest (204km per hr) is "Kingda Ka" at Six Flags New Jersey, USA.

11 Space

Three of the original five **Space Shuttles** remain in service, the first and only reusable space craft ever built. NASA's new spacecraft, called **Orion**, is due to come into service in 2010 – it may be used for manned missions to the Moon or Mars.

Bridges

The Akashi-Kaikyo suspension bridge in Japan, linking Kobe with Awaji Island, has the world's largest span at 1990.8m, while the Lake Pontchartrain Causeway, USA, is the longest bridge overall at 23.87 miles.

▸▸ Seven great bridges

Bosphorus Bridge, Turkey Completed in 1973, this 1560-metre-long suspension bridge was the first bridge linking Asia and Europe.

Brooklyn Bridge, USA Iconic link between Manhattan and Brooklyn, New York, and on completion in 1883 it was the largest suspension bridge in the world (main span 486.3m)

Forth Bridge, Scotland This 2.5-kilometre-long cantilever rail bridge was hailed as an engineering marvel in 1890, connecting Edinburgh with Fife in Scotland.

Humber Bridge, England At 1410m long, this was the largest suspension bridge in the world from 1981 to 1998.

The Iron Bridge, England Crossing the River Severn in Shropshire, this was the world's first cast iron bridge on its completion in 1779.

Sydney Harbour Bridge, Australia The world's largest single-arch bridge and an Australian icon, completed in 1932 with a total length of 1149m.

Verrazano-Narrows Bridge, USA Connecting the New York City boroughs of Brooklyn and Staten Island, this great span stands sentry to the harbour, and is the starting point of New York's marathon every year.

13 Seven underwater wonders

Blue Grotto, Capri, Italy Long discovered by travellers, but a beautiful spectacle nonetheless, with daylight refracted through the water as the purest azure blue.

Deep sea vents, Pacific Ocean, Red Sea Submarine hydrothermal vents lie at the bottom of the ocean, often accompanied by vast "chimneys" of rock and up to 300 species of marine life.

Galapagos Islands, Ecuador Home to some of the most unusual marine life on the planet.

Great Barrier Reef, Australia The world's largest reef system, stretching 2600km along the east coast of Australia, comprising over 900 islands and almost 3000 individual reefs.

Lake Baikal, Russia Deepest and oldest lake in the world – it contains 20% of all fresh water on Earth with a maximum depth of 1637m, and is packed with unique aquatic life, including the Baikal seal.

Lofoten Islands Maelström, Norway The confluence of currents just off this chain of Norwegian fjords creates a whirlpool that fired the imagination of Edgar Allen Poe, amongst others.

Palau, North Pacific Tiny island nation surrounded by rich waters teeming with over 500 species of fish and 700 types of coral.

Worship

The world's largest Christian church is the Basilica of Our Lady of Peace of Yamoussoukro in Côte d'Ivoire (30,000 square metres), a little larger than St Peter's Basilica in the Vatican City, Rome (23,000 square metres). The Faisal Mosque in Islamabad, Pakistan, is the world's largest (5000 square metres), while the largest synagogue is Temple Emanu-El in New York (3523 square metres).

15 Mountains

Mount Everest (or Mount Qomolangma in Tibetan) is the world's highest mountain (8848m) and was first conquered in 1955 by Sherpa Tenzing Norgay and Edmund Hillary. Today around 150 climbers make the ascent each year and thousands visit Base Camp, prompting environmentalists to call it "the highest junkyard in the world".

Volcano

The world's largest active volcano is Mauna Loa (4169m), while the most active is Kilauea (continuously erupting since 1983), both in Hawaii. Mauna Loa last erupted in 1984. Mount St Helen's eruption in 1980 (in Washington state, USA), created the world's largest landslide.

16 Transport

Ever since the creation of **Titanic**, ocean liners have been one of the grandest man-made sights on earth. Today's behemoths of the ocean include the world's largest cruise ship, *Queen Mary 2* (345m long), and the largest ship, oil container *Jahre Viking* (458m long).

On land, it's all about speed. The Maglev **train** connecting Shanghai with its international airport travels at an average 431km per hour, while the fastest recorded time by a train was 515kph by France's TGV.

17 The Internet

The Internet is widely regarded as the greatest invention of the modern era: over one billion people are thought to access the net on a regular basis, and search engine Google receives around one billion requests per day.

According to the UK newspaper *The Guardian*, the Seven Wonders of the Web are:

- Google — www.google.com
- Yahoo — www.yahoo.com
- Project Gutenberg — www.gutenberg.org
- Multimap — www.multimap.com
- Ebay — www.ebay.com
- Amazon — www.amazon.com
- Blogger — www.blogger.com

"Science fiction does not remain fiction for long. And certainly not on the Internet."

Vinton Cerf

18 Tallest buildings

Taipei 101 (508m) in Taiwan is the world's highest building, although the CN Tower in Toronto, Canada, is the tallest tower at 553.34m, and the KVLY TV Tower in North Dakota (629m) is the tallest structure overall. The Burj Dubai ("Dubai Tower"), on completion in 2008, may take all these titles at an eye-popping 800m high.

19 Art

The most expensive painting ever sold was Picasso's *Garçon à la Pipe*, bought for US$104m at Sotheby's in New York in 2004 by a private buyer.

"I don't say everything, but I paint everything."

Pablo Picasso

20 The movies

Titanic (1997) made a staggering US$1.834bn at the box office, though if adjusted for inflation, *Gone with the Wind* (1939) would have netted over US$5bn at today's prices. The largest movie screen is at the Panasonic IMAX theatre at Darling Harbour, Sydney, measuring 35.72m by 29.57m.

21 Airplane graveyard

One of the most surreal sights anywhere on the planet lies just outside Tucson, Arizona, where the Davis Monthan US Air Force Base stores around 4000 obsolete military aircraft.

22 Energy

The world's largest concentration of wind turbines is at Altamont Pass wind farm, California, with 7500 turbines smothering the hills along Interstate 580.

23 Surf's up

Cortes Bank, 100 miles off the coast of California, is reputed to produce the world's biggest waves: Mike Parsons rode a 18-metre-high wave off the bank in 2001, after being towed out by jet ski.

24 Seven ancient wonders

Most people have heard of the seven wonders of the ancient world, but no one knows who complied the original list. What is known is that it was first mentioned in Herodotus's *Histories* as early as the fifth century BC, and that the list was re-compiled in the middle ages – by which time at least some of the wonders had been lost. Today only the pyramid at Giza remains.

Ancient Wonder	Location
Great Pyramid of Giza	Egypt
Hanging Gardens of Babylon	Babylon (Iraq)
Temple of Artemis at Ephesus	Turkey
Statue of Zeus at Olympia	Greece
Mausoleum of Maussollos at Halicarnassus	Turkey
Colossus of Rhodes	Greece
Lighthouse of Alexandria	Egypt

25 Seven modern wonders

Following the Greek list of "Seven Wonders" created in the second century BC (see below), there's been fierce debate over what would appear on an updated version: the American Society of Civil Engineers came up with a widely quoted version in 1994.

Channel Tunnel UK/France

The 31-mile tunnel's innovative design includes three 1.5-metre-thick concrete tubes, the broadest trains ever built (double deckers), and three hundred miles of cold water piping alongside the tracks.

CN Tower Toronto, Canada

The world's tallest tower (553.34m) was erected incredibly quickly (5.5m per day), with the seven-storey SkyPod put together around the base and jacked up the tower in one piece.

Empire State Building New York, USA

At 381m, the Empire State Building was the tallest building in the world from 1931 to 1972, and remains an iconic skyscraper. Construction was completed in just one year and 45 days.

Golden Gate Bridge San Francisco, USA

With a total length of 2.7km and main span of 1280m, the bridge was the world's longest between 1937 and 1964, and remains the symbol of San Francisco.

Itaipu Dam Brazil/Paraguay

Spanning the Parana River and five miles wide, the main dam is 65 storeys high, using enough iron and steel to construct three hundred Eiffel Towers.

North Sea Protection Works Netherlands

This unique and complex system of dams, floodgates and storm surge barriers protects the Netherlands from the North Sea. The main features are a 19-mile-long dam to block the Zuider Zee, and the Eastern Schelde Barrier, two miles of gates between huge concrete piers.

Panama Canal Panama

The largest canal and lock system in the world, completed under the direction of George Washington Goethals by 42,000 workers, the Panama Canal is 77km long and took ten years to complete (1914).

COLOSSVS SOLIS.

Ultimate experiences Wonders of the World small print

ROUGH GUIDES – don't just travel

We hope you've been inspired by the experiences in this book. There are 24 other books in the 25 Ultimate Experiences series, each conceived to whet your appetite for travel and for everything the world has to offer. As well as covering the globe, the 25s series also includes books on **Journeys, World Food, Adventure Travel, Places to Stay, Ethical Travel, Wildlife Adventures** and **Wonders of the World**.

When you start planning your trip, Rough Guides' new-look guides, maps and phrasebooks are the ultimate companions. For 25 years we've been refining what makes a good guidebook and we now include more colour photos and more information – on average 50% more pages – than any of our competitors. Just look for the sky-blue spines.

Rough Guides don't just travel – we also believe in getting the most out of life without a passport. Since the publication of the bestselling Rough Guides to **The Internet** and **World Music**, we've brought out a wide range of lively and authoritative guides on everything from **Climate Change** to **Hip-Hop**, from **MySpace** to **Film Noir** and from **The Brain** to **The Rolling Stones**.

Publishing information

Rough Guide 25 Ultimate experiences Wonders of the World Published May 2007 by
Rough Guides Ltd, 80 Strand, London WC2R 0RL
345 Hudson St, 4th Floor,
New York, NY 10014, USA
14 Local Shopping Centre, Panchsheel Park,
New Delhi 110017, India
Distributed by the Penguin Group
Penguin Books Ltd,
80 Strand, London WC2R 0RL
Penguin Group (USA)
375 Hudson Street, NY 10014, USA
Penguin Group (Australia)
250 Camberwell Road, Camberwell,
Victoria 3124, Australia
Penguin Books Canada Ltd,
10 Alcorn Avenue, Toronto, Ontario,
Canada M4V 1E4
Penguin Group (NZ)
67 Apollo Drive, Mairangi Bay, Auckland 1310,
New Zealand

Printed in China

80pp
A catalogue record for this book is available from the British Library
ISBN: 978-1-84353-835-6

1 3 5 7 9 8 6 4 2

Rough Guide credits

Editors: Keith Drew, Martin Dunford
Additional contributions: Philippa Hopkins
Design & picture research: Diana Jarvis
Cartography: Katie Lloyd-Jones, Maxine Repath
Cover design: Diana Jarvis, Chloë Roberts
Production: Aimee Hampson, Katherine Owers
Proofreader: David Paul

The authors

Keith Drew (Experiences 1 and 8) is a Rough Guides editor and enthusiastic traveller to South America.

Stephen Keeling (Experiences 2, 6, 7 and 16, Miscellany) is the author of the Rough Guide to Taiwan and a contributor to the Rough Guides to Spain and Mexico.

Michael Haag (Experience 3) is the author of the Rough Guide to the Da Vinci Code and writes regularly about Egypt and the Middle East.

James Read (Experience 4) is the author of the Rough Guide to Bolivia and a contributor to the Rough Guide to South America

Martin Zatko (Experience 5) is writing the Rough Guide to Korea and his Slovak-Irish-Polish ancestry makes him eminently qualified to write about Turkey.

Brendan Griffen (Experience 9) has contributed to Rough Guides on Spain, Portugal, West Africa, Central America and Bolivia.

Andrew Benson (Experience 10) splits his time between Argentina and Europe and has co-authored or contributed to several Rough Guides, including Argentina and Chile.

Martin Dunford (Experience 11) is a co-founder of Rough Guides and has authored Rough Guides to Brussels, Amsterdam, New York, Rome and Italy.

Andy Turner (Experience 12) is a Rough Guides editor and keen traveller.

Karoline Densley (Experience 13) is a Rough Guides editor and co-author of the Rough Guide to Amsterdam. She has travelled extensively throughout Australasia.

Jonathan Buckley (Experience 14) is the author of the Rough Guide to Venice, co-author of the Rough Guides to Tuscany & Umbria and Florence, and has also published four novels.
Chris Scott (Experience 15) is an author, tour leader and film-maker with extensive knowledge of the Sahara, after more than 20 expeditions there in the last 25 years. He is co-author of the Rough Guide to Australia, and author of Sahara Overland.
Nikki Birrell (Experience 17) is a Rough Guides editor and keen traveller.
Rob Coates (Experience 18) is a contributor to the Rough Guide to Jamaica and keen traveller to the Caribbean and Central America.
Nick Edwards (Experience 19) co-authors the Rough Guide to India and lives in Pittsburgh, where he is a member of the Peace Movement and a big Spurs fan.
Jean McNeil (Experience 20) writes the Rough Guide to Costa Rica and is co-author of the Rough Guide to Central America. She has also won several awards for fiction writing.
Melissa Graham (Experience 21) has travelled widely in Chile, Peru and Ecuador, and co-authors the Rough Guides to Chile and Ecuador.
Emma Gregg (Experience 22) writes the Rough Guide to Gambia and contributes to numerous magazines and guidebooks, including the Rough Guide to West Africa.
Andrew Rosenberg (Experience 23) heads up the Rough Guides US editorial team and makes regular pilgrimages to Las Vegas.
Simon Lewis (Experience 24) is the author of the Rough Guide to Beijing and co-author of the Rough Guide to China.
Paul Smith (Experience 25) is a contributor to the Rough Guide to South America

Picture credits

Cover Sphinx, Giza, Egypt © Guy Midkiff/Alamy
8-9 Salar de Uyuni salt desert © TORRIONE Stefano / Hemispheres Images/Alamy
10-11 Detailed view of the Uluru © Bertrand Collet/iStock; Detailed view of Uluru © Hideo Kurihara/Alamy
12-13 Cheop's Pyramid © AKG-Images/Pearson; Giza Pyramids, Egypt © Corbis/Bettmann/ Pearson
14-15 Vine on a Tree © Philip Puleo/iStock Aerial view of the Amazon river © Johnny Lye/iStock; Man rowing on Amazon River © Chris Sanders/Getty; Spider in Amazon © Philip Puleo/iStock; Blue Morpho Butterfly from the Amazon Rainforest © Steve Geer/iStock; Common Squirrel Monkey in the tree canopy © Valerie Crafter/iStock; Red parrot feather from the Amazon © Steve Geer/iStock
16-17 Hot Air Balloon near Goreme © tbkmedia. de/Alamy; Uchisar Castle Cappadoccia © Murat Baysan/iStock; Strange stone formations, Cappadoccia © Svetlana Tikhonova/iStock
18-19 Mather Point on the South Rim of the Grand Canyon © Tom Till/Alamy
20-21 The Treasury, Petra © Robert Harding World Imagery/Pearson; Coloured sandstone in Petra © Peter Arnold, Inc./Pearson
22-23 Machu Picchu © Vladimir Korostyshevskiy/ iStock; Llama at Machu Picchu © Rough Guides Machu Picchu © Tomasz Resiak/iStock; View trough Machu Picchu window © Marketa Ebert/iStock
24-25 Sagrada Famila, Barcelona © Hamish Barrie/iStock; Gaudi Sculptures on Sagrada Famila Façade © Ken Sorrie/iStock; Sagrada Scaffolding © Marc C. Johnson/iStock; Sadness and Pain © Alison Cornford-Mattheson/iStock Rapture © Marco Crisari/iStock
26-27 Walking on the Perito Moreno Glacier © Mark Shenley/Alamy; Crevasse of blue ice on Perito Moreno Glacier © Vick Fisher/Alamy
28 Detail from the Last Judgement ©Vatican Museums and Galleries, Vatican City, Italy/The Bridgeman Art Library
28-29 The Creation of Adam © Vatican Museums and Galleries, Vatican City, Italy/The Bridgeman Art Library; Sistine Chapel Ceiling: Drunkenness of Noah © Vatican Museums and Galleries, Vatican City, Italy/The Bridgeman Art Library
30-31 The Machapuchare Mountain Peak, Nepal © Mountain Light Photography, Inc./ Pearson
32-33 Angkor Wat, Cambodia ©Getty Images/ Digital Vision/Pearson; Giant face at Bayan Temple, Angkor Wat © Jeremy Edwards/iStock; Ta Phrom Aspara, Angkor Wat © Jeremy Edwards/iStock

34–35 The Grand Canal Venice © Diana Jarvis
36–37 Berber camel train at sunrise © Carl Jani/iStock
38–39 The Great Wall © Awie Foong/iStock Great Wall at Jinshanlin © Chris Ronneseth/iStock; Great Wall of China © Erich Chen/iStock Great Wall at Badaling seen through archway ©Ed Freeman/Getty; Great Wall of China, visitors walking on carriageway to tower © Colin Sinclair/DK/Pearson; Army soldier photographs his girlfriend on the Great Wall of China © Tom Stoddart Archive/Getty
40–41 Couple kissing by Victoria Falls © Nikki Birrell; Bungy jumping off Victoria Falls Bridge © Chad Ehlers/Alamy; Victoria Falls, Zambia, View from Royal Livingstone © James Scully/iStock
42–43 Man kayaking towards little island, Placencia, Belize © Mark Lewis/Getty
44–45 The carved columns and filigree marble screens of the Red Fort in Agra framing the domes of the Taj Mahal beyond ©AA World Travel Library/Alamy
46–47 Temple V Steps at Tikal © Astrida Valigorsky/iStock; Maya Temple at Palenque, Chipas, Mexico © nikada33/iStock; Mayan relief showing King Pakal and his Mother, Palenque © Alexander Wilms/iStock; Yucatan, Bonampak murals © Rough Guides
48–49 The massive moai of Ahu Tongariki Rapa Nui Chile © Micele Falzone/Alamy
50–51 People working on restoring and applying the Grand Mosque with fresh mud © Yadid Levy/Alamy: Mali the desert close to Timbuktu © Hemis/Alamy
52–53 Paris Las Vegas Hotel Casino © Jon Arnold Images/Alamy Venetian gondola, Las Vegas © iridescent/iStock; New Luxor hotel Las Vegas © Barry Lewis/Alamy: New York New York Hotel and Casino in Las Vegas Nevada © Wesley Hitt/Alamy; Trippy Roulette Wheel © Steve Harmon/iStock
54–55 Detail of Door Forbidden City Beijing China © Wendy Connett/Alamy; China, Beijing, the Forbidden City © Yann LAyma/Getty
56–57 Hydroelectric power station Itaipu dam Parana River, Brazil © mediacolor's/Alamy
72 Engraving of the Colossus of Rhodes by Martin Heemskerck © Bettmann/CORBIS